You Think You Know Everything, You Don't Know How Wrong You Are

The Book of General Ignorance, exposing the Truth Behind Common Myths and Misconceptions

DAVID BOBKER

CONTENTS

FOREWORD

There are so many ways the world around you is not what you think it is. After all, the world is a strange place and it's growing more bizarre every day. Our world is made even stranger when we find out that beliefs and things we've held dear for ages, are not what we think they are.

But don't worry, this book will set the record straight on all the common myths that most people take for fact, making you the most well-informed person in town. So next time someone proclaims that Napoleon Bonaparte was short, or that shaving causes hair to grow back thicker, you can correct them, and tell them smugly that everything they think they know is wrong.

This book is a collection of common myths and misconceptions and the truths behind them which few people around us aware of. It may turn some of your thoughts about the world upside down, from law, history, religion, science, to body, food, mind, sport and nature.

The book will give you a look at the world around you in a completely new light and you will soon realize that everything you think you know about the world is wrong.

-1-
BODY AND MIND

For as long as we've had bodies and minds capable of thinking about these bodies, we've thought wrong things. Obviously, we're always learning and improving, but some misconceptions persist. Perhaps it's time to do away with a few of these.

Different tongue parts

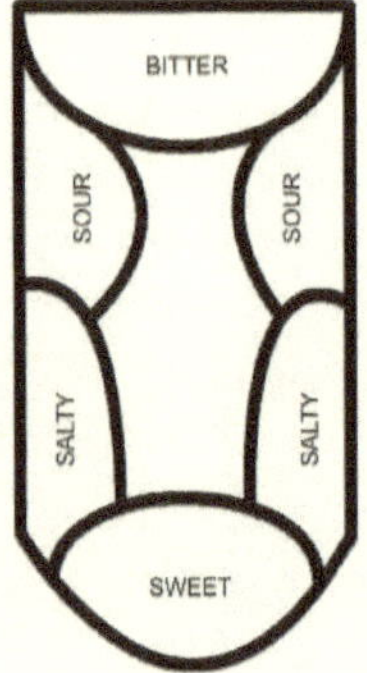

Everybody has seen the tongue map – that little diagram of the tongue with different sections neatly cordoned off for different taste receptors. Sweet in the front, salty and sour on the sides and bitter at the back.

It's possibly the most recognizable symbol in the study of taste, but it's wrong. In fact, it was debunked by chemosensory scientists (the folks who study how organs, like the tongue, respond to chemical stimuli) long ago.

The ability to taste sweet, salty, sour and bitter isn't sectioned off to different parts of the tongue. The receptors that pick up these tastes are actually distributed all over.

Body heat and the head

We all are reminded to cover our heads to stay warm. One of the reasons we do this is because of the age-old theory that we lose approximately half of our body heat through our heads, but is this bit of advice really true?

The origin of this belief comes most likely from an old U.S. Army Field Manual from the 1950 which is based on arctic survival research. The problem with the study is that while the research was performed on subjects wearing cold weather gear, they were not wearing hats. Naturally, in circumstances like this, body heat will escape from whatever area is exposed – in this case, the subjects uncovered heads.

Since our heads represents only 10% of our body's total surface area, it would have to lose about 40 times as much heat per square inch as other parts of the body for this theory to be true. In fact, only in infants is most heat lost through the head, or if the head is the only uncovered part of the body.

Even though there is no factual basis to the concept of losing excess body heat through our heads, most will agree that if you want to stay warm this winter, you should cover your entire body to prevent heat from escaping…including your head.

Don't eat and swim

The old saying that you should wait at least 30 minutes after eating before you swim is based on the idea that after a big meal, blood will be diverted away from your arms and legs, towards your stomach's digestive tract. And if your limbs don't get enough blood flow to function, you're at risk of drowning.

 It's true that digestion redirects some of the blood from the muscles to aid in the digestive process. With a reduced blood flow, there is potentially less oxygen available to the working muscle and stomach, which is a potential cause of cramping – though some researchers discount this theory.

The truth is we have enough blood to keep all our body parts functioning after a big meal. It doesn't increase risk of cramps; alcohol is the biggest risk increaser. But a full stomach will make you short of breath. With any vigorous exercise after eating, there could be some discomfort such as heartburn or vomiting, caused by unexpected reflux or involuntary regurgitation. This is more likely to occur when there's an increase in external pressure, such as while diving.

Milk increases mucous

The belief has been held for years that milk causes mucus formation, although the few studies on this topic have failed to demonstrate any effect of milk on mucus production. Many people confuse the temporary, slight thickening of saliva after drinking milk with mucus. There is no scientific research showing that milk produces mucus in the airways or the throat. It will not worsen cold or asthma symptoms. In fact, although many people reduce milk intake when they have a cold, one clinical trial showed milk and dairy food intake was not associated with an increase in upper or lower respiratory tract symptoms of congestion. Studies have found milk intake was not associated with increased nasal secretions, coughing, nose symptoms or congestion. Some doctors say that milk thickens saliva, which may coat the throat and give the perception of more mucus, but it does not cause the body to produce more mucus or phlegm.

Furthermore, milk may actually contribute to speeding up recovery, as drinking lots of fluids when you have a cold is important. Frozen dairy foods and fruit smoothies may soothe a sore throat and provide important calories and nutrients when you are not eating much else.

Shaving thickens hair

Shaving your hair - no matter what part of your body — doesn't mean the hair will grow back faster or thicker.

The roots of this myth may be tied to the fact that hair regrowth can look different at first.

Unshaven hair has a finer, blunter tip. When you experience hair regrowth, you'll see the coarser base and not the softer, thinner part that will eventually grow back (if you let it get that far).

New hair may also look darker. This is partly due to its thickness, but it may also be because the new hair hasn't yet been exposed to natural elements. Sun exposure, soaps, and other chemicals can all lighten your hair.

The dark shade of hair regrowth may also be more noticeable than you're accustomed to. If you have lighter skin, you may notice new hairs even more. This all has to do with the color contrast. It isn't attributed to the shaving process whatsoever.

However, shaving can still lead to side effects. These are most likely attributed to improper shaving techniques. Possible side effects include: skin irritation, razor burn, contact dermatitis, cuts, ingrown hairs, blisters, pimples, itchy skin.

Caffeine dehydrates you

It is true that caffeinated drinks can contribute to your daily fluid requirement.

Drinking caffeine-containing beverages as part of a normal lifestyle doesn't cause fluid loss in excess of the volume ingested. While caffeinated drinks may have a mild diuretic effect — meaning that they may cause the need to urinate — they don't appear to increase the risk of dehydration.

Still, caffeinated drinks can cause headaches and insomnia in some people. Also, some studies suggest that if you're pregnant, high levels of caffeine consumption could increase your chance of preterm birth or miscarriage. Water is probably your best bet to stay hydrated. It's calorie-free, caffeine-free, inexpensive and readily available.

Alcohol keeps you warm

The characteristic flushed cheeks and occasional sheen of sweat on someone who's been imbibing certainly suggest that alcohol has an effect on body temperature, but when you drink an alcoholic beverage, does it really warm you up?
The culprit behind that warm, fuzzy feeling you get after a few drinks? Blood. Many side effects from alcohol consumption can be tied to its properties as a vasodilator (blood vessel widener), including the so-called "beer blanket" phenomenon. "[Alcohol] causes the blood vessels in your skin to dilate, shunting blood from your core to your periphery," said Ted Simon, a neuroscientist and board-certified toxicologist who serves as an expert witness in drug and alcohol cases.

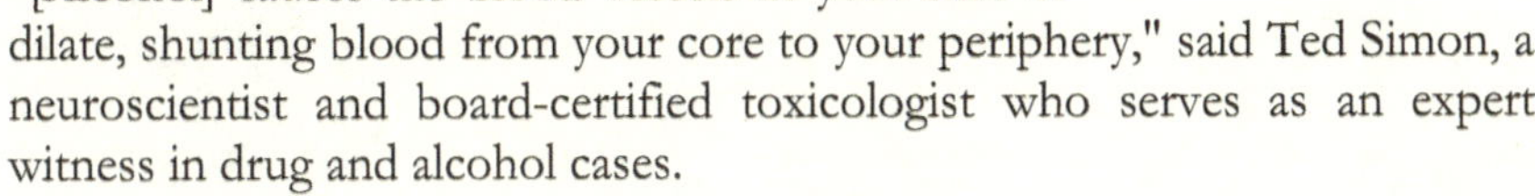

Your body temperature isn't changing. It's only you're just redistributing the heat.

Alcohol kills brain cells

Just one observation of a drunken person is enough to convince you that alcohol directly affects the brain. People who drink enough to get drunk often end up with slurred speech and impaired motor skills and judgment, among other side effects. Many of them suffer from headaches, nausea and other unpleasant side effects afterward -- in other words, a hangover. But are a few drinks on the weekend, or even the occasional long drinking session, enough to kill brain cells?

Not so much. Even in alcoholics, alcohol use doesn't actually result in the death of brain cells. It can, however, damage the ends of neurons, which are called dendrites. This results in problems conveying messages between the neurons. The cell itself isn't damaged, but the way that it communicates with others is altered. According to researchers such as Roberta J.Pentney, professor of anatomy and cell biology at the University at Buffalo, this damage is mostly reversible.

Chewing gums take 7 years to digest

Although chewing gum is designed to be chewed and not swallowed, it generally isn't harmful if swallowed. Folklore suggests that swallowed gum sits in your stomach for seven years before it can be digested. But this isn't true. If you swallow gum, it's true that your body can't digest it. But the gum doesn't stay in your stomach. It moves relatively intact through your digestive system and is excreted in your stool.

On very rare occasions, large amounts of swallowed gum combined with constipation have blocked intestines in children. It's for this reason that frequent swallowing of chewing gum should be discouraged, especially in children.

Waking sleepwalkers is dangerous?

It is a myth that it is dangerous to wake up a sleepwalker because it may cause them a heart attack, shock, brain damage, or something else. It is not a myth that it is dangerous to wake up a sleepwalker because of the possible injury the sleepwalker may inflict upon themselves or the person waking them up.

According to Dr Giuseppe Plazzi of the Department of Neurological Sciences at the University of Bologna in Italy, rousing a sleepwalking person, especially vigorously, might confuse or distress them temporarily. Disoriented, they may strike out at anyone close. It is best not to be in their way.

Instead, it might be better to simply guide them back to bed in their sleep. It is not likely that a sleepwalker when woken up suddenly will have a cardiac event. It is no different from when a person sleeping normally is suddenly awakened by, say, a loud noise. The important thing is to protect a sleepwalker from themselves.

If awoken, a sleepwalker of any age isn't in danger of losing their soul or suffering brain damage. However, waking them could trigger a stress response with unintended consequences for either you or the sleepwalker. The startle response can increase activity in the amygdala, which plays a role in emotional responses like fear or anxiety. When startled, the sleepwalker will act out in a manner like a fight or flight response. They may lash out or fall, which could injure them or the person waking them. According to Wright, it is best to gently encourage or lead a sleepwalker back to bed and let them get on with their night's rest.

Sugar: Does it really cause hyperactivity?

The sugar-hyperactivity myth is based on a single study from the mid 1970s in which a doctor removed the sugar from one child's diet and that child's behavior improved. Since then, over a dozen larger studies have been conducted and not one of them has found that sugar causes hyperactivity. Interestingly enough, researchers have found that parents are more likely to say that their kids are overly active when they think they've consumed sugar. In one study, parents were asked to rate their child's hyperactivity after consuming a drink with sugar. Unknown to the parents, the drink was sugar-free, but the parents still rated their child as more hyperactive.

Studies have disproves this. ADHD (Attention-deficit hyperactivity disorder) and poor behaviors still occurs in children with sugar-free diets. Even though most kids don't have a sugar sensitivity, that doesn't mean sugar is good for their health. Sugary foods and beverages deliver calories without any nutrients. What's more, eating foods high in added sugars throughout childhood is linked to the development of risk factors for heart disease, such as an increased risk of obesity and elevated blood pressure in children and young adults.

Vaccine cause autism

Autism, or autism spectrum disorder (ASD), refers to a broad range of conditions characterized by challenges with social skills, repetitive behaviors, speech and nonverbal communication. According to the Centers for Disease Control, autism affects an estimated 1 in 59 children in the United States today.

Some people have had concerns that ASD might be linked to the vaccines children receive, but studies have shown that there is no link between receiving vaccines and developing ASD. In 2011, an Institute of Medicine (IOM) on eight vaccines given to children and adults found that with rare exceptions, these vaccines are very safe.

A study added to the research showing that vaccines do not cause ASD. The study looked at the number of antigens (substances in vaccines that cause the body's immune system to produce disease-fighting antibodies) from vaccines during the first two years of life. The results showed that the total amount of antigen from vaccines received was the same between children with ASD and those that did not have ASD.

Left and Right brain

The left-brain right-brain myth stems from the common idea that your dominant personality traits are related to which side of your brain has more control. Supposedly, left-brained people are more logical, while right-brained people are more creative. This popular idea has been around for

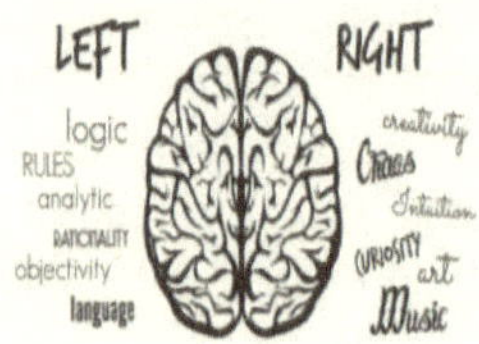

more than 200 years and has proliferated in the age of BuzzFeed personality quizzes, but it simply isn't true. In reality, people use both sides of the brain equally, and logic and creativity are not mutually exclusive.

It's true each hemisphere of the brain controls different functions, but this fact doesn't relate to personality. The misleading idea of left- vs. right-brained people originates from science and has become fictionalized over time. No solid division between talents of each hemisphere; left brain can learn 'right brain' functions and vice-versa.

Do people only use 10% of their brains

The human brain is complex. Along with performing millions of mundane acts, it composes concertos, issues manifestos and comes up with elegant solutions to equations. So it's no surprise that the brain remains a mystery unto itself.

Adding to that mystery is the contention that humans "only" employ 10 percent of their brain. If only regular folk could tap that other 90 percent, they too could become savants who remember to the twenty-thousandth decimal place or perhaps even have telekinetic powers.

Certainly there is no truth to the idea that we only use 10 percent of our neural matter. Modern brain scans show activity coursing through the entire organ, even when we're resting. Minor brain damage can have devastating effects - not what you'd expect if we had 90 percent spare capacity. Also, consider the situation when neural tissue representing a limb is rendered redundant by the loss of that limb. Very quickly, neighboring areas recruit that tissue into new functions, for example to represent other body regions. This shows how readily the brain utilizes all available neural tissue.

-2-
FOOD

We all tend to believe what we hear or read from the health enthusiasts and fitness experts. Food is one arena which is filled with many myths and misconceptions. While some may be true to some extent, some others are outright lies.

Salty water boils quicker

Amateur chefs everywhere seem to swear by it, and some professional chefs do too. You put your spiffy new pot full of water on the stove, fire up the burners, and just as it's heating up, you toss a pinch of salt in to speed up the process to boil some delicious pasta. In fact, adding salt does the very opposite of making water boil faster. Instead, it makes it take longer for the water to boil! The salt actually increases the boiling point of the water, which is when the tendency for the water to evaporate is greater than the tendency for it to remain a liquid on a molecular level.

When the salt is added, a phenomenon known as "boiling point elevation" is put into effect, which involves those old chemistry mainstays—the solute, solvent, and solution. Boiling point elevation happens when a non-volatile solute (or a dissolvable substance—in this case, the salt) is added to a pure solvent (or a substance that dissolves a solute—in this case, the water itself) to create a solution (the salt water).

The salt water requires more exposure to the heat in order to boil than water alone, so the boiling point is elevated and the time it takes to get the water to boil increases. This makes the water hotter (the new boiling point is increased to about 216° F, as opposed to the standard 212° F for unsalted water), but it still doesn't make it boil faster.

White sugar is bad, brown sugar is good

When we visit our favorite cafes, we tend to choose brown sugar over white sugar because it is a good alternative. We buy into the myth that it is healthier than white sugar. But that is not the case. Brown sugar contains very small traces of minerals that they are of no actual benefit to us. You should understand that brown sugar is also sugar in the end and would lead to the same kind of calorie consumption and the resulting health issues.

Low fat makes for a healthy meal

We all have come to hear from the health gurus to our neighbors that low fat content makes for a healthy meal. You have to know that not all low-fat meals are healthy. Many products like flavored yogurt and snacks which are advertised as such are full of salts and sugars. Also certain fats (Monounsaturated fats) like those found in avocados and nuts are pretty healthy. They not only help in weight loss but also help in lowering cholesterol and making your heart strong. It all depends on the nutritional value of the meals, including the quantity of fat.

Natural means healthy

Just as a low-fat label does not automatically signal a
healthy snack, neither does an "organic" or "natural"
one. Although organic foods may be healthier than
non-organic versions of the same snack, being
organic or natural does not exclude foods from
being loaded with salt, sugar or saturated fats.

Organic food

Also, be wary of labels that state foods "contain" organic or natural
ingredients, as very often this does not mean much at all. A fruit-flavored
product, for example, may claim it contains real fruit, but this doesn't mean
there is any substantial amount in the product - or indicate what the rest of
the ingredients are. Although it is good to eat naturally and organically
where possible, it is also important to check labels to make sure "natural"
products are really as healthy as they seem.

Being organic or natural does not exclude foods from being loaded with
salt, sugar or saturated fats.

Bottled water is better than tap water

We are constantly encouraged to drink more water for our health, and a
common misconception is that drinking it by the bottle is a much healthier
way of doing this. While there has been no scientific evidence that bottled
water is better for us, some studies have actually suggested it is worse.

The Natural Resources Defense Council (NRDC) did a four year review of
the bottled water industry and found the water to be no safer or healthier,
findings that were also confirmed in a separate study by the University of
Geneva. The NRDC further concluded that 25 per cent of the water they
tested was in fact just tap water in a bottle. Studies have also suggested that
bottled water may be worse for our health as chemicals (phthalates) from
the bottles leak into the water over time, which may lead to hormone
imbalance when consumed in high levels.

While there are some definite advantages (primarily in terms of convenience
and taste) to choosing bottled water, in our opinion, the drawbacks seem to
outweigh those advantages. Bottled water is far more costly and hazardous
to the environment for us to be able to recommend it as the better option.

Craving is your body's way of saying it needs something

A big misconception about food cravings is that they are our body's way of telling us we are lacking a certain nutrient and need to remedy this immediately via a huge slab of chocolate cake (or your particular food of choice). However, while this theory may help ease our guilt over giving in to cravings, it has yet to be proven true, and more recent research has suggested that food cravings are in fact all in the mind.

A study published in the journal Appetite has suggested that many people crave the foods that they attempt to resist the most, such as junk food. Research has also suggested that people simply crave the foods that they are most exposed to and familiar with, which is demonstrated by the fact that most people crave sugary, salty and fatty foods. Your body and mind will only crave the foods they remember, meaning that eating a healthy, balanced diet - with a little of what you fancy - should help to reduce those junk food cravings.

Late-night eating will make you fat

It is a common misconception that eating late in the evening or too close to bedtime will make you gain weight. The logic behind this myth is that the energy from your late-night dinner or bed-time snack will get stored as fat while you sleep, but that is not how it works according to research explained by the BBC.

Binging on high-sugar, high-fat foods causes you to go to bed with elevated blood sugar levels. At any time of day, these set the body up for subsequent sugar crashes and weight gain, with the body quickly storing excess sugar as fat, says Lori Zanini, a California-based registered dietitian and certified diabetes educator with HealthCare Partners medical group. But, since your body uses less sugar as fuel when you're lying in bed as opposed to running around, potentially more sugar winds up in your fat cells when you eat those foods late at night.

The body doesn't care when you consume your calories. It only cares about how many calories you consume and just as importantly how many you burn. If you consume more calories than you burn you will gain weight. And if you burn more calories than you take in every day you will lose weight. It is that simple.

Eating carrots will improve your vision

Everyone grows up thinking eating carrots help keep their eyes healthy, whether that's improving your eyesight or just keeping your already-great vision strong.

 Carrots are high in vitamin A, a nutrient essential for good vision. Eating carrots will provide you with the small amount of vitamin A needed for good vision, but vitamin A isn't limited to rabbit food; it can also be found in milk, cheese, egg yolk, and liver. So eating more carrots won't help improve your vision if you are getting enough vitamin A in your diet. The funny thing is even though they're super good for your body and contain eye-boosting vitamin A, Harvard Medical School says eating fresh fruits and dark leafy green veggies are even better, more beneficial choices when it comes to your eye health.

Milk builds strong bones.

One of the major ingredients for healthy bones is calcium. This mineral provides structural strength to bones and teeth, and helps the body perform numerous other functions, such as clot blood and transmit nerve impulses. Normally, your body gets the calcium it needs from your diet, but if that's not possible, it'll start pulling calcium from your bones, making them weaker in the process.

In the United States, milk has become synonymous with strong bones. It's long been a recommendation by doctors and the U.S. Department of Agriculture that everyone over 8 years old include three cups of dairy in their diet every day. But over the years, experts have poked some holes in the milk-bone health connection.

Despite getting served a carton of milk with your school lunches and all those "Got Milk?" ads that promise strong bones, milk isn't as good for you as it's advertised to be. A 2010 study published in the journal Nutrition in Clinical Practice found milk might be the reason bones lose calcium, doing the opposite of what it promises to do. On top of that, a 2009 study published in the American Journal of Clinical Nutrition discovered the rates of bone fractures were highest in the countries that consumed the most dairy. Interesting, right? Maybe it's time to make the switch to soy or almond after all.

Vitamin C can keep you from catching a cold

Research has shown that vitamin C generally does not ward off colds, but it may be helpful in people who participate in extreme physical exercise. A 2019 study in the Journal of the International Society of Sports Nutrition found ingesting a pill of ascorbic acid, or vitamin C, before a single bout of exercise suppressed superoxide dismutase activity, a marker of stress in the body, among participants who took the pill, compared with those who ingested a placebo. However, the researchers are unclear on the efficacy of vitamin C supplementation on exercise-induced oxidative stress.

The most convincing evidence to date comes from a 2013 review of 29 randomized trials with more than 11,000 participants. Researchers found that among extremely active people—such as marathon runners, skiers, and Army troops doing heavy exercise in subarctic conditions—taking at least 200 mg of vitamin C every day appeared to cut the risk of getting a cold in half. But for the general population, taking daily vitamin C did not reduce the risk of getting a cold.

Avoid eggs because of their cholesterol content

Chicken eggs are an affordable source of protein and other nutrients. They're also naturally high in cholesterol. But the cholesterol in eggs doesn't seem to raise cholesterol levels the way other cholesterol-containing foods do, such as trans fats and saturated fats.

Eggs have gotten an unfounded bad rap; in a 2018 study in the journal Nutrients, researchers found eggs don't actually contribute to high cholesterol. In fact, eggs are an inexpensive source of many nutrients, including zinc and iron, antioxidants lutein and zeaxanthin, vitamin D, and the brain-boosting chemical choline. However, keep in mind that the research on eggs has gone back and forth over the years so don't overdo it. The American Heart Association says one whole egg or two egg whites a day can be part of a healthy diet. Keep cholesterol in check by monitoring saturated fat in your diet.

If you like eggs but don't want the cholesterol, use only the egg whites. Egg whites contain no cholesterol but still contain protein. You may also use cholesterol-free egg substitutes, which are made with egg whites.

-3-

SPORT

There's the myth that lightning never strikes twice in the same place. And then there's the myth about Tomatoes being a wonderful, tasty, healthy, nutritious vegetable. In the sports industry, there's many sporting myths which although are commonly practiced and preached around the world are just as wrong as our beliefs about lightning and tomatoes.

Gold medals are made of gold

It seems winning a gold medal isn't as rewarding as we once believed.

Comprised of 1.34 percent gold, 93 percent silver and six percent copper, this "gold" medal earns $650 when melted down and sold at market value.

Might as well hand the winner a painted can of corn and call it a day.

No sex before the game

No evidence sex impairs athletic performance. It could even help athletes due to increased testosterone.

Clearly, a lot of men believe that sex and sports don't mix—but do they have any real reason to be worried? Will a pre-competition roll in the hay necessarily drain your strength? According to a new study published in *The Journal of Sexual Medicine*, this fear doesn't seem to be based in reality.

In the study, researchers at California State University, San Marcos provided the first-ever data looking at whether previous-day sex affects the amount of muscle force men can exert with their legs the following day. They studied 12 healthy young men (age 25 on average) who had their leg strength and endurance tested twice: once on a day when they had sex the night before, and again on a day when they had abstained from sex the previous night. The exercises the men engaged in focused specifically on quadriceps and hamstring torque.

Black belts are masters

While obtaining a black belt in the martial arts is a huge accomplishment, the recipient is not a master of the art. In fact, the rank is just the beginning of the journey towards mastery.

In many styles of martial arts, it takes four to five years to obtain the rank of black belt, which in Japanese is called "shodan." This translates to "first step." A student who earns a black belt has learned their basic blocks, kicks, and punches. He or she has become proficient in the self-defense aspects of the art in which they practice. Yet, there is still much to master.* Just like a student who graduates from high school, additional training is needed to gain a more in-depth understanding of the subject.

Training doesn't stop after achieving the rank of first-degree black belt. Many students work their way up to a second-degree black belt, third-degree black belt, and so on. They recognize that there is still much to learn mentally and physically even after they first tie their black belt around their waists.

Only muscle soreness makes the training effective

Muscle soreness is not an indication of the effectiveness of the training. Rather, it is a sign of overstraining the structures. The pain has nothing to do with an excess of lactic acid, but the pain is caused by small injuries in the muscle fibers. Muscle soreness "may occur" nevertheless never train consciously for minutes in the pain range on a muscle soreness. If you continue to exercise despite sore muscles, the tissue can scar and be damaged in the long term. Especially the aching muscle groups should be spared until they are completely regenerated. Muscle ache is "normal", especially for beginners, bur even professionals can feel it during unusual exercises. However, it becomes dangerous if aching muscles are caused by the wrong training technique. Therefore, check your execution regularly and get help from trainers and experts.

The only way to learn to love a sport is to specialize early and focus on getting better in that sport.

Early specialization may lead to a greater risk for burnout due to stress, decreased motivation and lack of enjoyment.

Research suggests that athletes can actually benefit from playing multiple sports by decreasing risk of overuse injuries and developing complementary skills. Consider the football player who had a higher chance of sustaining a shoulder injury had he not had a break from football during the baseball season, or the soccer player who developed the muscular strength and coordination necessary to avoid a serious knee injury by learning to jump as a basketball player. Had you asked these athletes to specialize early in life, the statistics tell us that at least one of them would have dropped out of sport completely due to burnout.

This sounds great hypothetically, but do these cases actually exist? Yes, they do. New England Patriots quarterback Tom Brady was drafted by the Montreal Expos out of high school. Olympic gold medalist soccer player Mia Hamm played football, basketball and baseball as a youth. Eight-time NBA All-Star Steve Nash grew up playing soccer and didn't even start playing basketball until age 12. Those are just a few of the current sports stars who grew up playing multiple sports.

Sports Are At Least "90% Mental" At Higher Skill Levels.

Yogi Berra, the legendary baseball great, was known to once say, "Baseball is 90% mental -- the other half is physical." So much for mathematical science. It is true that in the upper levels of a sport, the mental game becomes more critical. After all, beginners in a sport are simply struggling to achieve a basic competence in physical skills. Thinking about complex game strategies and competitive psychological issues are the least of their concerns.

Another common statistic (spoken with such conviction as to sound downright scientific) thrown around is that humans use only 10% of their brain power. How can anyone possibly measure or prove a statement like this? Because these percentage-based statements are impossible to verify, they add little credible discourse to sport psychology.

Here, though, is one never-ending oddity. If at least 90% of all athletes and coaches state that the mental arena is vital, and absolutely critical at the higher reaches of a sport, then why do they also admit that they rarely practice mental skills? Perhaps they don't know how to practice these skills, or are not psychologically minded enough to seek assistance in this area. There still remains, in many sports, a stigma associated with an athlete who is "too mental". That's unfortunate.

Sports Psychology Is Only For Athletes Who Are Mentally Weak.

The term "mentally weak" implies there is an inherently defective or temporarily fragile mental quality in an athlete. This is not a helpful or accurate statement, as many elite athletes who are quite mentally strong still seek the services of sport psychologists on a regular basis. This is one of the most pervasive and damaging of the many myths about sport psychology. Think for a moment.

Why does Tiger Woods continuously have a golf coach on his staff? His game is not "weak or broken". He works with a coach so he can continue to improve, and to minimize any backsliding. The same is true with athletes who seek the services of sport psychologists. They want to improve their mental skills.

Athletes Are Overpaid

Sticking with the angry mother for a moment, let's look at that last line again. She specifically brings up how much money Can Newton makes, as if that justifies her complaint. Athletes have long dealt with the "overpaid" stigma hanging over their head. When they make a mistake, they're told "you make millions of dollars to do one thing and you can't get it right."

The reality couldn't be farther from the truth. Sticking with Cam Newton, he makes $20.76 million on average, per season. In a vacuum, that does admittedly sound like a lot to throw a ball around. But you need to take into consider what he means to the team. He's a superstar, taking the team to 12-0 right now without anyone on offense to help him. If the Panthers didn't pay him that much, someone else would have.

Oh, and the Carolina Panthers are worth an estimated $1 to $1.5 billion depending on your source. Even then, that's 19th overall in the NFL, the most profitable sport in the country. To them, to the whole NFL, $20 million would be the equivalent to you or me buying a new TV. Yeah, it's a bit pricey, but we can easily afford it and it's a great investment.

College Athletes Are Always Given Full Scholarships

In reality, there's a lot of moving parts to college scholarships. The first thing is that the chances of getting a scholarship is super rare. Yes, all the big names get one, but while those big name athletes get all the headlines, the majority of college athletes have to pay their own way. On average, only 2% of high school students get a scholarship and, even then, it's generally for about $11,000.

Then there are the so called "head-count sports," the sports where athletes are given a full ride scholarship or none at all. These sports include football, men's and women's basketball, gymnastics, volleyball, and tennis. Notice baseball, golf, and soccer aren't on that list? The athletes in these "head-count" sports get a 100% full ride or not a single penny. If a student athlete is injured the school isn't required to pay for the medical care. At the University of Maine for example, the athlete is responsible for the first $10,000 in deductibles and co-payments. Not to mention the athlete is on the hook if the injury persists after they graduate.

-4-
LAW

We are somewhat accustomed to regard ourselves as being free from the superstitions and prejudices of our forefathers, yet it is probable that the present generation has inherited a number of these, besides generating quite as many misconceptions of fact as any that have preceded it.

Missing person reports

Missing persons reports are a popular story component on crime and legal shows but in real life the situation is much more dramatic. By the time a missing persons report is filed, tensions are often running high and that can mean important details are missed.

Many shows and movies have publicized the 24 or 48 hour waiting period to report missing people but that doesn't exist in real police offices. As soon as you know an adult or child is missing, report it to police. Police don't demand a 24-hour period before accepting a missing persons report.

"Yes, I'm a cop"

US undercover police do not have to identify themselves as cops. Police not only can lie to you, they will lie to you in order to get what they want: an arrest

Although undercover stings may seem like entrapment, courts do not see it that way. In the legal sense, entrapment only occurs when a cop induces someone to commit a crime that the person would otherwise not have committed. If you are unlucky enough to be busted by an undercover cop, the courts will simply assume that you would have committed the "crime" with another person; this will fatally undermine any entrapment defense.

Remember, police will lie to you in order to get their way. Police are under no obligation to follow through on their promises, even if you hold up your end of bargain by cooperating. Cooperating only increases the chances that you will incriminate yourself, while having no effect on criminal sanctions.

Winning a case is all about the legal technicalities.

Winning a case is more often about common sense persuasion. While there are notable exceptions to this, generally the law in civil courts is designed to produce equitable outcomes. The initial stages of a case can be full of technicalities, especially in the Motion to Dismiss stage, but especially once you get to a jury trial, the jury will be full of people just like you and me. They're sworn to do their best to enforce the law, but they also want to see justice done. A lawyer once said, "If the jury feels you deserve to win, they will drape the law over you to ensure you do." We do believe that inside each of us is a moral compass. We know fundamentally what is fair and what is not fair. The law is designed to uphold those principles.

You'll be a great lawyer if you're good at arguing

Law practice can be intellectually rigorous, but much of a lawyer's work is actually mundane and repetitive. New lawyers, especially those in large firms, are often charged with the mind-numbing tasks of document review, cite checking, and routine research.

Litigation is an adversarial process, but legal advocacy is not about "arguing" in the traditional sense of the word. It's not about engaging in a verbal battle with your opponent, but rather persuading your audience—judge, mediator, or jury—through a logical, well-researched, well-reasoned discussion based on the facts and the law.

Law is a trade, not a business.

Law firms are profit-seeking businesses. Law firms are highly hierarchical. Partners at law firms are responsible for bringing in clients, and their relative value at their law firm depends on their status as a "rainmaker." Therefore, they spend most of their time selling. The vast majority of legal work is done by associates, or alternatively, service partners, who do not hold equity stake in the law firm and are paid on a salaried basis. As a client, this means that aligning your incentives with the law firm's incentives is tremendously important.

If your law firm has "skin in the game" and upside to be gained from winning your case, they will consciously or unconsciously cut down on costs and seek to maximize gains. When we fund cases, we always look for skin in the game from the law firm involved.

Making partner at a top law firm is about being the best lawyer.

Making partner at a top law firm is about bringing in business. When you go to law school, you study case law and civil procedures. But in practice, law firms operate much more like traditional businesses than like heroic movie montages starring Atticus Finch or Clarence Darrow. The truth is, law firms reward people who bring their own book of business. That means young lawyers have to either mine their own contacts for clients or alternatively, establish good relationships with older partners in order to inherit their book of business. If you're coming out of law school, the most important thing for you to know is not how to try a case, but rather, how to get a client.

"I don't need to form a business entity if I am the only employee."

If you do not conduct business under a properly formed legal business entity, such as a corporation or LLC, you can be held personally liable for your business debts and creditors can take your individual property, such as your home, to satisfy these debts. If operated properly, having a legally formed business entity can protect your individual assets in the event of a problem.

"If I form a business entity, nobody can take my personal assets."

While forming a corporation, LLC, or other business entity makes it more difficult for creditors to go after your personal assets, it does not guarantee that your personal assets are safe. Creditors may be able to take your individual property if you co-mingle your business and personal finances, or if you do not follow legal corporate formalities. It is important to operate your business and personal finances separately to protect your personal assets.

Parents are responsible for the negligent acts of their children.

While this statement may seem logical, it is untrue. Parents are not responsible for the consequences of their children's negligent conduct. If, however, the parents own conduct is negligent, then the parent can be held responsible for their own actions.

As an example, the child finds a firearm in the woods and negligently discharges it, causing property damage or personal injury. A parent would not be responsible for those acts. However, if the same child found a loaded hand gun in their home that the parent negligently failed to secure and the child discharges that firearm, causing property damage or personal injury, the parent could be held responsible for their own actions in negligently failing to secure the firearm. Liability or responsibility for negligent acts can most often be insured against and most homeowner's policies include children of the named insured, provided that they are residents of the household. Automobile insurance policies have their own unique coverages, and parents should from time to time review their insurance coverages for their homeowner's coverage and automobile coverage regarding the protection not only for themselves but for their children.

-5-
NATURE

Head outside with kids and you'll probably find yourself tempted to share advice bestowed on you when you were small. But have you ever wondered if the "wisdom" passed down by your elders is actually correct?

Electric fan at night

Scorching summer days can be tough without air conditioning, and you might find yourself searching for ways to stay cool, including using a fan at night. But is it healthy to sleep with a fan on? Some recent headlines have made sleeping with a fan on sound downright dangerous. "Why Sleeping with Your Fan on Could Be Seriously Damaging Your Health. "Sleeping with a Bedside Fan Could Pose Health Risks". But experts say the reality is not that dire. It's very unlikely to harm you.

If you do sleep with a fan on, Horovitz said it's a good idea to keep it at a safe distance from your bed and not have it blowing right on you. To guard against dust and other allergens, Horovitz recommended keeping an air filter in the bedroom. He also recommended performing daily sinus irrigation with saline, which can help with dry nasal passages, congestion and other nasal problems.

Sharks = No cancer

Scientists have known for more than 150 years that sharks get cancer. And yet the belief persists that the animals don't suffer from the disease.

This misconception is promoted in part by those who sell shark cartilage, who claim that the substance will help cure cancer, said David Shiffman, a shark researcher and doctoral student at the University of Miami. But no studies have shown that shark cartilage is an effective treatment, and the demand for the material has helped decimate shark populations, researchers say: Humans kill about 100 million sharks per year, according to a March 2013 study (although many factors contribute to the killing of sharks, including demand for shark-fin soup).

It's unknown what caused the tumors in the great white or bronzer shark. However, reports of cancerous tumors in marine animals, especially mammals, have steadily increased over the past 20 years, raising concerns that industrial pollutants or human activities may trigger the cancers, according to the study. Beluga whales have been recorded to suffer from cancer, and in areas near aluminum smelting plants, cancer is the second leading killer of the whales, the study noted.

Bulls hate red

Bullfighting conjures a common image: An angry bull charging at a matador's small red cape, the *muleta*. But, why does the beast charge at the sight of red?

Actually, it doesn't. Bulls, along with all other cattle, are color-blind to red. Thus, the bull is likely irritated not by the *muleta*'s color, but by the cape's movement as the matador whips it around. In support of this is the fact that a bull charges the matador's other cape — the larger *capote* — with equal fury. Yet this cape is magenta on one side and gold or blue on the other.

It appears that bulls get irritated by the cape's movement, not its color. The television show Mythbusters tested this hypothesis during one of their shows. Their tests showed that bulls had the same reaction to white capes and blue capes as they did to red capes. Moreover, their tests revealed that bulls only became interested and began charging the capes when they were moved around.

Great Wall of China

One popular myth about space exploration is that the Great Wall of China is the only human-built structure that can be seen from space. But this is not true. The reality is that you can't easily see the Great Wall with the unaided eye, even from low Earth orbit. And certainly, the Apollo astronauts couldn't see it from the Moon, even though that urban legend has been widely circulated. Additionally, when China's first astronaut, Yang Liwei, went into space in 2003, he said that he couldn't see the structure of the Great Wall from out his capsule window.

NASA has confirmed that US astronaut Leroy Chiao took what is thought to be the first verifiable image of the Great Wall of China from out his window on the International Space Station in 2004, using a zoom lens. He photographed a region of Inner Mongolia, about 200 miles north of Beijing, but said Chiao himself said he didn't see the wall with his unaided eyes, and wasn't sure if the picture showed it.

The Apollo astronauts confirmed that you can't see the Great Wall of China from the Moon. In fact, all you can see from the Moon is the white and blue marble of our home planet.

With all of the human construction, many buildings and other structures can be seen from space. But you can't see the Great Wall of China from space.

Bananas grow on trees

Do you think bananas grow on trees? Wrong. They don't, because the banana tree is actually a plant. It is probably the largest plant in the world. Bananas actually grow on massive herbs that resembles trees.

At the top of the plant is a chunk of leaves looking like a palm tree. The flower bud grows in the stalk, which is right in the middle of these leaves. From this flower bud grows the bunch of banana fruits, all of which point skywards. There is only one bunch at a time. But, it can be quite heavy. Sometimes, it could weigh up to 45 kilograms!

Dogs sweat by salivating

No. They regulate temperature through panting. They actually sweat through footpads.

Dogs have two types of sweat glands: Merocrine glands, apocrine glands. Merocrine sweat glands function similarly to human sweat glands. These glands are located in your dog's paw pads and activate when he is hot to cool him down. This is why you might notice damp paw prints on the ground during particularly hot days. Most dogs are covered in fur, so sweat would fail to evaporate from their bodies. That's why it is much more efficient for dogs to have sweat glands in their paw pads, where there is little fur.

Apocrine sweat glands are different from merocrine. While veterinarians consider them to be sweat glands, their main purpose is to release pheromones, not cool your dog off. These glands are located all over your canine companion's body and help him identify other dogs by scent, kind of like human body odor.

Bats are blind

Contrary to what most people believe, bats are generally not blind at all and in fact are believed to have eyesight keener than that of most humans. The misconception that bats are blind comes from their nocturnal nature and enhanced hearing abilities. Because they hunt mostly in the dead of night, when lighting conditions are, of course, very dark, bats rely on echolocation to pinpoint exact locations of prey. This ability does not, however, require or have any connection to blindness. Instead, the genetic mutations that evolved the powers of echolocation in bats likely surfaced as they aided the animals in the darkness. A bat's eyes, far from useless, are attuned to low-light conditions to better aid in finding prey and are enhanced by their super hearing power.

Don't touch baby birds

Wrong, says Miyoko Chu, a biologist at the Cornell Lab of Ornithology. "Birds don't have a very strong sense of smell," she said, "so you won't leave a scent that will alarm the parent."

In fact, contrary to what our parents may have told us, most bird parents are unlikely to abandon their chicks over a little human fiddling. "Usually, birds are quite devoted to their young and not easily deterred from taking care of them," Chu said.

But before you put on your Bird Rescuer costume and start saving the day, Chu suggests you shouldn't go around picking up every baby bird you see. Baby birds may look stranded when in fact their parents are hiding close by. In fact it's very common for young birds to leave the nest before they're ready to hit the skies.
"If you back up and watch them," Chu said, "in a lot of cases the parent will come back and feed the young and protect it."

And your handling of the bird might be doing more harm than good, said Tom Hahn, an ornithologist at the University of California in Davis. "A much bigger risk to the babies, if humans mess around with them, is that the activity of the human around the nest may attract the attention of predators, which may subsequently come get the babies," he says.

We have 5 senses

Humans have way more than five senses, and if you include the animal kingdom there even more still.

Scientists say there are far more, but disagree on the exact number. Most of those familiar with the matter say there are between 14 and 20, depending on how you define a sense. Perhaps the simplest definition is: a sense is a channel through which your body can observe itself or the outside world.

Even those senses we humans are familiar with aren't always so straightforward when you dig a little deeper. At least not for everyone. Consider synesthesia, a rare condition where a person experiences a blending of two senses. The most common variety is grapheme-color synesthesia, which is where each particular number or letter corresponds with a certain color or shade. A rare number of savants actually use this ability to make advancements in mathematics or music composition.

MSG = headaches

Monosodium glutamate (MSG) is the sodium salt of an amino acid found

naturally in our bodies called glutamic acid. Some people have a sensitivity to MSG that results in a headache and other symptoms. First identified as "Chinese-restaurant syndrome" in 1968, further research suggests the culprit is MSG.

Scientists have been unable to link MSG to headaches and other symptoms conclusively. Regardless, many people commonly report MSG as a headache or migraine trigger, and researchers acknowledge that a small percentage of people may have a short-term reaction to the additive.

The mechanism behind MSG-induced headaches is not fully understood. MSG is an excitatory amino acid that binds to MNDA receptions in the brain. This activation leads to the release of nitric oxide, which then leads to the dilation or widening of blood vessels around the skull.

Goldfish has 3-sec memory

Most goldfish keepers will have heard the "fact" that goldfish memory spans are just three seconds long — but is it true? Scientists have proven that goldfish memory spans are nowhere near as short as three seconds. Your goldfish can actually remember things for at least five months.

If goldfish memory was just three seconds long then they would not be able to remember that pressing the lever dispensed food or that the sound meant food was available.

Human and Dinosaurs

Many believe that dinosaurs and humans once coexisted, but most know that current technology doesn't allow for cloning dinosaurs from fossils.

A latest research shows that 41% of Americans think that dinosaurs and humans either 'definitely' (14%) or 'probably' (27%) once lived on the planet at the same time. 43% think that this is either 'definitely' (25%) or 'probably' (18%) not true while 16% aren't sure. In reality the earliest ancestors of humans have only been on the planet for 6 million years, while the last dinosaurs died out 65 million years ago.

There is a religious split on this question. While most Americans who describe themselves as 'born again' (56%) believe that humans and dinosaurs once shared the planet, most Americans who do not describe themselves as born again (51%) think that they did not. Only 22% of born again Americans think that dinosaurs and humans did not coexist.

Glass is a liquid

In medieval European cathedrals, the glass sometimes looks odd. Some panes are thicker at the bottom than they are at the top. The seemingly solid glass appears to have melted. This is evidence, say tour guides, Internet rumors and even high school chemistry teachers, that glass is actually a liquid. And, because glass is hard, it must be a supercooled liquid.

Glass, however, is actually neither a liquid—supercooled or otherwise—nor a solid. It is an amorphous solid—a state somewhere between those two states of matter. And yet glass's liquidlike properties are not enough to explain the thicker-bottomed windows, because glass atoms move too slowly for changes to be visible.

When glass is made, the material (often containing silica) is quickly cooled from its liquid state but does not solidify when its temperature drops below its melting point. At this stage, the material is a supercooled liquid, an intermediate state between liquid and glass. To become an amorphous solid, the material is cooled further, below the glass-transition temperature. Past this point, the molecular movement of the material's atoms has slowed to nearly a stop and the material is now a glass. This new structure is not as organized as a crystal, because it did not freeze, but it is more organized than a liquid. For practical purposes, such as holding a drink, glass is like a solid, Ediger says, although a disorganized one.

-6-
RELIGION

Being misunderstood is no fun in any context but when it is about something so personally meaningful as religion or non-religion, it can be infuriating.

Fatwa = death sentence

People make assumptions about what things are and what words mean on the basis of the available information. If someone doesn't know anything about islamic law and hears about issuing a fatwa implying issuing a death sentences in the news, and never hears about any other sorts of fatwas, then it is not very surprising that they think that a fatwa involves a death sentence. And since there is no great international interest in more mundane fatwas, their hypothesis hasn't come into contact with falsificatory evidence. It's nothing as grand as a fallacy or bias.
It actually means 'non binding legal opinion'. The best-known sort of fatwa in the West is that which calls for the death of a blasphemer; e.g., the fatwa by Ayatollah Ruhollah Khomeini of Iran pronouncing a sentence of death against Salman Rushdie in 1989. For this reason, some Westerners believe the word "fatwa" to be a synonym for "death warrant."

Satan rules Hell

There is a common misconception that Satan is in charge of hell and that he and his demons live there and use their pitchforks to torment souls for eternity. This concept has no basis in Scripture whatsoever. In fact, Satan will be one of the tormented in the lake of fire, not the tormentor (Revelation 20:10).

Where does the idea that Satan is the master of hell come from, if not from the Bible? Much of the false thinking may come from Dante Alighiere's epic poem The Divine Comedy. Many other works of art, and literary pieces such as Dan Brown's novel Inferno, follow Dante's lead and picture Satan as the one in charge of hell.

Jihad is "Holy war"

Satan does not rule hell or lead his demons in tormenting those who are banished there. In fact, the Bible does not say that Satan has been to hell yet. Rather, "eternal fire" is awaiting Satan; the place was originally created to punish Satan and the demons (Matthew 25:41), not to give them a kingdom to rule.
"Jihad" appears to have become the scariest word in the world these days. This month, Muslim activist Linda Sarsour used the word in a lecture — expressing her hope that God accepts the efforts of Muslims to peacefully resist anti-Muslim discrimination in the United States as a form of jihad.

Contrary to what extremists and anti-Muslim personalities claim, the word "jihad" does not mean "to wage holy war," or "to kill the infidel," or "to commit terrorism." The word "jihad" means "to struggle." The prophet Muhammad said the best jihad was to speak words of truth "in front of a tyrannical leader" — and this is what Sarsour clearly referenced in her lecture. Not violence. Not terrorism. Indeed, the only two groups who claim "jihad = Terrorism" are Islamic State terrorists and Islamophobes with an agenda. Both are ignorant of Islam and serve only one another.

The Three Wise Men

The Bible does not say that exactly three magi came to visit the baby Jesus, nor that they were kings, or rode on camels, or that their names were Casper, Melchior, and Balthazar. The three magi are implied because three gifts are described but we only know that they were plural (at least 2 magi) but could have been many more and probably included an entourage accompanying them on their journey. The artistic depictions of the nativity have almost always depicted three magi since the 3rd century.

The Bible only specifies an upper limit of 2 years for the interval between the birth and the visit (Matthew 2:16), and artistic depictions and the closeness of the traditional dates of December 25 and January 6 encourage the popular assumption that the visit took place in the same season as the birth, but later traditions varied, with the visit taken as occurring up to two years later. The association with kings comes from efforts to tie the visit to prophecies in the Book of Isaiah

Martyrs and 72 virgins

The Quran does not promise martyrs 72 virgins in heaven. It does mention companions, houri, to all people—martyr or not—in heaven, but no number is specified. The source for the 72 virgins is a hadith in Sunan al-Tirmidhi by Imam Tirmidhi. Hadiths are sayings and acts of the prophet Mohammed as reported by others, and as such they are not part of the Quran itself. Muslims are not meant to necessarily believe all hadiths, and that applies particularly to those hadiths that are weakly sourced, such as this one. Furthermore, the correct translation of this particular hadith is a matter of debate.[80] In the same collection of Sunni hadiths, however, the following is judged strong (hasan sahih): "There are six things with Allah for the martyr. He is forgiven with the first flow of blood (he suffers), he is shown his place in Paradise, he is protected from punishment in the grave, secured from the greatest terror, the crown of dignity is placed upon his head—and its gems are better than the world and what is in it—he is married to seventy two wives among Al-Huril-'Ayn of Paradise, and he may intercede for seventy of his close relatives."

All Religions Are Essentially the Same

The 'nice' form of this secular myth says that all religions teach the same (nice) ethics. The strident 'New Atheist' version of this myth says that all religions are just as bad as each other – they're abusive, and 'poison everything'.

Now, to be fair, there are some similarities between various religions: many of them *ask similar* questions. However, they often come up with *different answers*. And it's the answers that matter. Poet Steve Turner nailed this in his sarcastic poem writing:

"We believe that all religions are basically the same,
at least the one that we read was.
They all believe in love and goodness.
They only differ on matters of
creation sin heaven hell God and salvation."

Religion is Merely a Private Belief, that Doesn't Impact a Person's Outward Behavior.

According to this myth, religion is nothing more than private *internal* beliefs, which don't impact a person's *outward* behavior. These religious beliefs might affect what worshippers do in a church/synagogue/mosque/temple one hour a week. But outside the four walls of their worship gathering, there are no significant behavior changes. In this narrative, Islamic terrorists (for example) are not motivated by their particular religious views, but by cultural, economic, and political reasons (e.g. perceived western oppression). But again, this secular view is a myth.

Our deeply held beliefs about morality, meaning, and purpose – the issues religions deal with – also drive behavior. An Islamic terrorist might believe that Allah calls upon him to bring death to infidels via the sword or suicide vest.

Religion is Against the Public Good

This view has been popularized by 'New Atheist' thinkers like Richard Dawkins and Christopher Hitchens. It re-appeared last year in MSM articles about the SSM postal survey. Fairfax columnist Aubrey Perry wrote:
"It's our opportunity to say that religion has no part in the shaping of our

laws. A vote against same-sex marriage is a vote for religious bias and discrimination in our legislation, our public schools, our healthcare, and ultimately, in the foundation of our social structure."

Religion – at least in it's traditional forms – is bad for society as a whole, according to this narrative. But does this view stack up? Is religion a force for evil in society – is it bad for human flourishing? The evidence is in, and overwhelmingly religion – at least the Christian religion – has been shown to be a positive influence in society.

Christianity is not about what we do for God but what he has done for us!

In order to please God or to earn God's favor all religions have rituals and sacred rules you must live by. Some religions (even 'Christian' ones) believe in doing good works to appease God, while others demand you make significant sacrifices in order to win Gods favor. Still others believe how you live this life determines what state you will live a following life in.

Christianity, on the other hand, is all about What Jesus Christ has done for us. Christianity teaches that there is nothing we can do to make ourselves right with God. We all fall short of Gods holy standard. However, the good news is, Jesus Christ made a way for us to be made right with God by giving his own life by dying on a cross. When you put your trust in Jesus Christ and what he has done for you, you are made right with God. Then Christians choose, not to appease God, but to live for him out of love for the One who gave his all for them.

Evolution and religion are incompatible.

The misconception that one always has to choose between science and religion is incorrect. Of course, some religious beliefs explicitly contradict science (e.g., the belief that the world and all life on it was created in six literal days); however, most religious groups have no conflict with the theory of evolution or other scientific findings. In fact, many religious people, including theologians, feel that a deeper understanding of nature actually enriches their faith. Moreover, in the scientific community there are thousands of scientists who are devoutly religious and also accept evolution.

SCIENCE

Even intelligent, educated people often get these science facts wrong. Here is a look at some of the most widely held scientific beliefs that simply aren't true. Don't feel bad if you believe one of these misconceptions—you're in good company.

Black hole is a hole

No, a black hole is not really a hole at all. A black hole is an object just like any other, except that it is extremely dense. This gives it such a high gravitational field that nothing, not even light, can escape. Because no light escapes a black hole, it is invisible – or 'black' – although they can be detected by their effect on the material around them. The term 'hole' was used because whatever falls 'into' a black hole is trapped forever.

Science fiction often depicts black holes as portals between different parts of the Universe, different times or different universes altogether. This may be why it is often misconstrued that black holes are 'holes' in space-time. This concept isn't entirely fictional, however

In 1935, Albert Einstein and Nathan Rosen proposed 'wormholes' through space-time, which could provide a means of traversing large distances instantaneously. But a naturally occurring black hole doesn't form a wormhole by default. In fact, there are doubts they could occur naturally at all, that they would remain stable for more than a fraction of a second or that they would be anything bigger than vanishingly small.

Is Evolution a 'theory'?

It seems clear that scientists can use the word "theory" to mean "conjecture," but it is also fair to say that typical circumstances, when scientists say "theory," they mean the hard usage of the term: "a more or less verified or established explanation." This thus leads to the question, under such a strong definition of the term, does evolution qualify as a theory?

Assuming that we are using the hard definition of theory, different people will give different answers to that question. Under such an understanding of the term, if we define theory as "a more or less verified or established explanation," then theory is in the eye of the beholder. Darwin-skeptics will not agree that neo-Darwinian evolution is "a more or less verified or established explanation." But Darwinists will agree. So the question over whether neo-Darwinian evolution should be called a "theory" is not the core question of this debate. A better question would be: "Is neo-Darwinian evolution 'a more or less verified or established explanation'?"

However, given that the technical, scientific, hard definition of theory does typically mean a well-established explanation and verified. Therefore, it is a complex question, for it can also depend on the definition of "evolution".

We evolved from chimpanzees

Chimpanzees (or other apes) didn't evolve into humans. Both lineages descended from a common ancestor and went their separate ways. The real question here is, who was that last common ancestor, the missing progenitor of both chimps and humans? We don't know yet.

Biologists have actually observed evolution happening in other species, both in the field and in the lab—the recent emergence of antibiotic-resistant microbes is a form of evolution. And animal breeders make evolution happen all the time—think of the tremendous variety of dog breeds that have been created from wolves. For a number of reasons, we share nearly 99 percent of our genetic sequence with chimpanzees and bonobos, which strongly suggests we share a common ancestor.

And there are thousands of fossils documenting progressively more human-like species in the evolution of our lineage after it split from the other great apes and later from chimps and bonobos.

Dropped pennies kill

There's a tale we've all heard: A penny dropped from the top of the Empire State Building would fall at such a rate it would impale and kill anyone it hit down below. The myth somehow weaseled its way through the generations, horrifying elementary school students and causing reasonable people to wonder if a day of New York City sightseeing would be their last.

But quietly, about a decade ago, University of Virginia physics professor Louis Bloomfield put those fears to rest by happily getting pelted with pennies from high above. For a penny to plummet at a lethal rate, it would need to fall in an airless environment. Bloomfield said a penny, or anything else, would hit the ground at a speed of about 210 mph if it were tossed from the Empire State Building in an airless environment. At that speed, Bloomfield said, anything, even a piece of paper, is dangerous. Bloomfield said a penny at 210 mph could break your skin if it hit you on its edge.

Items that are more aerodynamic or heavy, such as a ball point pen or bowling ball, may be able to cut through the air better. Both items, Bloomfield said, if dropped from the Empire State Building, would hit the ground at close to 210 mph.

Flushed water rotation

The idea that water rotates differently in the different hemispheres is a long-standing one. It sounds true. Just like Lisa explains to Bart (The Simpsons), the Earth is subject to Coriolis forces, which determine how moving objects are deflected off the inside of rotating objects—wheels, circular containers, those kinds of things. Applied to Earth's rotating sphere, the Coriolis effect accounts in part for why, say, hurricanes and cyclones rotate the way they do. (The storms rotate counterclockwise in the Northern Hemisphere and clockwise in the Southern).

Coriolis forces are best observed at a large scale; toilet water, in so many ways, is small-scale. As Robert Ehrlich, a physicist at George Mason University, explains it: "The effects of the rotation of the earth are, of course, much more pronounced when the circulation covers a larger area than would occur inside your bathtub." So what does account for the varying ways that toilets flush and drains drain? The design of the objects that do the flushing and the draining, for the most part. (Not to mention things like buildup and debris, which can affect the shape water takes as it's moving through pipes).

There Is a Dark Side of the Moon

Have you noticed that when you look up at the moon, you always see the same features? You can see craters and patches of different colors. With a pair of binoculars or a telescope, you can make out even more detail. But no matter how you look at the moon, you're always seeing the same landscape. What's on the other side of the moon?

Many people use the phrase "the dark side of the moon" to describe something mysterious and unknown. The dark side of the moon is supposed to be the side we never see, the side that faces away from Earth. This side of the moon faces the cold, black expanse of space. What could be on this side of the moon?

The moon rotates as it orbits the Sun, much like the Earth. While the same side of the moon always faces the Earth, the far side could be either dark or light. When you see a full moon, the far side is dark. When you see (or rather, don't see) a new moon, the far side of the moon is bathed in sunlight.

The North Star Is the Brightest Star in the Sky

Certainly the North Star (Polaris) is not the brightest star in the Southern Hemisphere, since it may not even be visible there. But even in the Northern Hemisphere, the North Star is not exceptionally bright. The Sun is by far the brightest star in the sky, and te brightest star in the night sky is Sirius.

The misconception likely arises from the North Star's use as a handy outdoor compass. The star is easily located and indicates the northern direction.

Lightning Never Strikes the Same Place Twice

If you have watched a thunderstorm any length of time, you know this is not true. Lightning can strike one place multiple times. The Empire State Building gets struck around 25 times each year. Actually, any tall object is at increased risk of a lightning strike. Some people have been struck by lightning more than once.

So, if it's not true that lightning never strikes the same place twice, why do people say it? It's an idiom intended to reassure people that unfortunate events rarely befall the same person the same way more than once.

Microwaves Make Food Radioactive

Microwaves do not affect the radioactivity of food.

Technically, the microwaves emitted by your microwave oven are radiation, in the same way visible light is radiation. The key is that microwaves are not *ionizing* radiation. A microwave oven heats food by causing the molecules to vibrate, but it does not ionize the food and it certainly does not affect the atomic nucleus, which would make food truly radioactive. If you shine a bright flashlight on your skin, it won't become radioactive. If you microwave your food, you may call it 'nuking' it, but really it's slightly more energetic light.

On a related note, microwaves do not cook food "from the inside out".

Venous Blood Is Blue

While some animals have blue blood, humans are not among them. The red color of blood comes from hemoglobin in red blood cells. Although blood is a brighter red when it is oxygenated, it is still red when it is deoxygenated. Veins sometimes look blue or green because you view them through a layer of skin, but the blood inside is red, no matter where it is in your body.

There are only three states of matter: solid, liquid and gas

Don't forget plasma. That makes four states. Plasma isn't some gel or goo, it's more like superheated ions and electrons. It's sometimes called "ionized gas." When cooled, it becomes gas, but then it takes on different properties, too. So it's not quite right to think of it as a kind of "gas." Plasma is more like a flame. Lightning, fire, the sun, and the tail of comets are all plasmas. Most any element or chemical compound can become plasma if heated high enough, but since plasma is just ions and electrons, the molecules have broken down. Water, for example, can be reduced to plasma, but it's no longer $H2O$; it's not even hydrogen or oxygen. And you definitely wouldn't want to drink it.

The conclusions of science are the propriety of scientists

The misconception that only scientists are qualified to understand, discuss or socially disposition a privation of science, and that the conclusions of scientists cannot be over-ruled by the public at large, at-risk stakeholders, nor their elected representatives. Science does not possess a method which substantiates it as a form of government.

"Fewer than 20% of those surveyed believe scientists are transparent about potential conflicts of interest with industry all or most of the time. The public is also skeptical that scientists regularly admit their mistakes." – Cary Funk, *Pew Research*

"We are not afraid to entrust the American people with unpleasant facts, foreign ideas, alien philosophies, and competitive values. For a nation that is afraid to let its people judge the truth and falsehood in an open market is a nation that is afraid of its people." – John F Kennedy

Because scientific ideas are tentative and subject to change, they can't be trusted.

Especially when it comes to scientific findings about health and medicine, it can sometimes seem as though scientists are always changing their minds. One month the newspaper warns you away from chocolate's saturated fat and sugar; the next month, chocolate companies are bragging about chocolate's antioxidants and lack of trans-fats. There are several reasons for such apparent reversals. First, press coverage tends to draw particular attention to disagreements or ideas that conflict with past views. Second, ideas at the cutting edge of research (e.g., regarding new medical studies) may change rapidly as scientists test out many different possible explanations trying to figure out which are the most accurate. This is a normal and healthy part of the process of science. While it's true that all scientific ideas are subject to change if warranted by the evidence, many scientific ideas (e.g., evolutionary theory, foundational ideas in chemistry) are supported by many lines of evidence, are extremely reliable, and are unlikely to change

The job of a scientist is to find support for his or her hypotheses.

This misconception likely stems from introductory science labs, with their emphasis on getting the "right" answer and with congratulations handed out for having the "correct" hypothesis all along. In fact, science gains as much from figuring out which hypotheses are likely to be wrong as it does from figuring out which are supported by the evidence.

Scientists may have personal favorite hypotheses, but they strive to consider multiple hypotheses and be unbiased when evaluating them against the evidence. A scientist who finds evidence contradicting a favorite hypothesis may be surprised and probably disappointed, but can rest easy knowing that he or she has made a valuable contribution to science.

Science is a collection of facts.

Because science classes sometimes revolve around dense textbooks, it's easy to think that's all there is to science: facts in a textbook. But that's only part of the picture. Science is a body of knowledge that one can learn about in textbooks, but it is also a process. Science is an exciting and dynamic process for discovering how the world works and building that knowledge into powerful and coherent frameworks.

There is a single Scientific Method that all scientists follow.

The Scientific Method" is often taught in science courses as a simple way to understand the basics of scientific testing. In fact, the Scientific Method represents how scientists usually write up the results of their studies (and how a few investigations are actually done), but it is a grossly oversimplified representation of how scientists generally build knowledge.

The process of science is exciting, complex, and unpredictable. It involves many different people, engaged in many different activities, in many different orders

-8-
HISTORY

History is a mishmash of real facts, exaggerations, and downright lies, and sometimes history is just something repeated over and over until people start believing it. Historical myths that aren't true but just won't go away.

Napoleon was short

Napoleon was 5'6" – 5'7" (168-170 cm) tall, which was slightly above average for Frenchmen of his time. The myth about Napoleon being short arose because the British liked to portray their French enemy as "little Boney". And since Napoleon was often surrounded by soldiers from his Imperial Guard, who were above average height, he appeared short in comparison. At his autopsy, Napoleon measured 5'2", but that was in French inches, which were larger than British and American inches.

Vikings' horned helmets

Forget almost every Viking costume you've ever seen. Yes, the pugnacious Scandinavians probably sported headgear when they marched into battle, but there's no reason to believe it was festooned with horns. In depictions dating from the Viking age—between the eighth and 11th centuries— warriors appear either bareheaded or clad in simple helmets likely made of either iron or leather. And despite years of searching, archaeologists have yet to uncover a Viking-era helmet embellished with horns. In fact, only one complete helmet that can definitively be called "Viking" has turned up. Discovered in 1943 on Gjermundbu farm in Norway, the 10th-century artifact has a rounded iron cap, a guard around the eyes and nose, and no horns to speak of.

The popular image of the strapping Viking in a horned helmet dates back to the 1800s, when Scandinavian artists like Sweden's Gustav Malmström included the headgear in their portrayals of the raiders. When Wagner staged his "Der Ring des Nibelungen" opera cycle in the 1870s, costume designer Carl Emil Doepler created horned helmets for the Viking characters, and an enduring stereotype was born.

Iron maidens are torture devices

The answer is no — and yes. The widespread medieval use of iron maidens is an 18th-century myth, bolstered by perceptions of the Middle Ages as an uncivilized era. But the idea of iron-maiden-like devices has been around for thousands of years, even if evidence for their actual use is shaky.

The iron maiden has been described as a human-sized box festooned with interior spikes. The hapless torture victim would be forced inside and the door would shut, driving the spikes into the body. The spikes were supposedly short and positioned so that the victim wouldn't die quickly, but would bleed out over time. Creepy, right?

And basically fictional. The first historical reference to the iron maiden came long after the Middle Ages, in the late 1700s. German philosopher Johann Philipp Siebenkees wrote about the alleged execution of a coin-forger in 1515 by an iron maiden in the city of Nuremberg. Around that time, iron maidens started popping up in museums around Europe and the United States. These included the Iron Maiden of Nuremberg, probably the most famous, which was built in the early 1800s and destroyed in an Allied bombing in 1944.

Einstein failed math

Underachieving school kids have long taken solace in the claim that Einstein flunked math as a youth, but the records show that he was actually an exceptional, if not reluctant, student. He scored high grades during his school days in Munich, and was only frustrated by what he described as the "mechanical discipline" demanded by his teachers. The future Nobel Laureate dropped out of school at age 15 and left Germany to avoid state-mandated military service, but before then he was consistently at the top of his class and was even considered something of a prodigy for his grasp of complex mathematical and scientific concepts. When later presented with a news article claiming he'd failed grade-school math, Einstein dismissed the story as a myth and said, "Before I was 15 I had mastered differential and integral calculus."

Ninjas wore only black

Ninjas were spies, assassins and covert agents – it wouldn't make much sense for them to wear something that would immediately give away their goals. They usually dressed as everyday folk or as other samurai. The popular idea of the black clothing wore by ninjas was probably borrowed from the puppet handlers of bunraku theater, who dressed in total black to simulate props moving independently.

However, ninjas were specialized in ambushes and quickly infiltrating and escaping areas at night, but even when they did use dark garments, they used dark blue and not black, because it blends better in the night. The Japanese Mikawa Go Fudoki describes a case of deception when ninja attackers used the same clothing as defenders, to instill confusion.

The pyramids were built by slaves

Slaves didn't build the pyramids of Egypt. The ancient Greek historian Herodotus once described the pyramid builders as slaves, propagating what became a global myth. Workers were likely poor people, but they were respected – pointed out by archaeologists who found their graves around or even inside the pyramids. There's no way they would be respected enough to be buried as slaves there.

Another myth regarding the pyramids is that they haven't changed since their construction. Initially, the great pyramids were covered with white limestone plated with gold – that outer coating has since washed away.

Benjamin Franklin discovered electricity

Benjamin Franklin made numerous scientific and political contributions in the world, but he didn't discover electricity. Egyptian scholars wrote texts in 2750 BC referring to electric fish as "the thunderers of the Nile," and several Mediterranean cultures were aware of static electricity. However, the first proper electrical study was conducted in 1600 by the English scientist William Gilbert who actually coined the term "electricity."

Benjamin Franklin had numerous contributions in the field, notably demonstrating the electrical nature of lightning using his famous kite experiment, at one point selling much of his possessions to fund his work.

Thomas Edison invented the light bulb

Contrary to popular belief, the light bulb, a mainstay of modern life, ubiquitous in the developed world, had been around years before Thomas Edison ever created one. Edison's contribution was to improve on it. Previous versions were unreliable, expensive, and didn't last very long. Up to 20 others independent inventors were doing the same thing as Edison at the time, trying to build a better light bulb. Edison's version of the light bulb improved on the filament, used a sealed vacuum bulb, and had a lower voltage than others at the time. The result was a marketable product that could last for hours. Edison's design has been improved upon over the years. Today standard incandescent bulbs can last for years, even this one that's still burning after 100 years! Stay tuned. Government rules have banned most incandescent bulbs due to their low efficiency. Light-emitting diodes produce light much more efficiently than incandescent bulbs and will one day supplant them.

Witches Were Burned at the Stake in Salem

Although there really were witch trials in Salem, Massachusetts, in 1692, and 20 people were put to death, none of the accused were burned at the stake. Hanging was the method of execution, although one victim was crushed to death under heavy stones.

Moreover, there's no evidence these people were practicing witchcraft or were possessed by the devil. Historians now believe that they, along with the townspeople who persecuted them, were suffering from mass hysteria. Others believe the accusers were afflicted with a physical illness, possibly even hallucinating after eating tainted rye bread.

Cinderella Wore Glass Slippers

Ask anyone and they'll tell you that Cinderella wore glass slippers to the ball, but historians say that part of the legend isn't true. More than 500 versions of the classic fairy tale exist, dating back as far as the 9th century. In each account, Cinderella has a magic ring or magic slippers made of gold, silver, or some other rare metal, which are sometimes covered with gems but are never made of glass.

In the earliest French versions, Cinderella wore *pantoufles en vair*, or "slippers of white squirrel fur." In 1697, when French writer Charles Perrault wrote "Cendrillon" his version of the tale, the word *vair* had vanished from the French language. Perrault apparently assumed it should have been *verre*, pronounced the same as *vair*, but meaning "glass." Even a wave of the fairy godmother's magic wand couldn't make that mistake disappear, and it has been passed down ever since.

Marie Antoinette said, "Let them eat cake."

Marie Antoinette never said, "Let them eat cake." The quote is commonly attributed to her, however it was actually from philosopher Jean-Jacques Rousseau's autobiography, *Confessions*, in which he recalls a story he once heard of a great princess who when told that the peasants had no bread replied, "Let them eat brioche."

It is unlikely that Rousseau could be writing about Marie Antoinette, as she was only 10 years old when his book was written in 1765.

History is the same as 'the past.'

It can be difficult to break this misconception, but a way to start is to ask your students to take a moment to think about everything that is happening around them; their internal thoughts and external choices, and their immediate surroundings. Now ask them to imagine the same for all the people currently alive; then the exchanges of all those people—every economic and social transaction—all the complex interactions and reactions occurring at that single second. Then ask them how future historians will write the history of this very moment: what will they choose to focus on? Ignore? How will they know and interpret this moment? What very real and important things might they miss?

Once a student understands that history and "the past" are different and that the past is so enormous and unknowable and historians piece together fragments of evidence to *interpret* (but not recreate) the past, then the foundation is already there for a much more fascinating exploration. "The past" has already happened, but how we view and learn from that past is very much alive—that's "history."

The Vomitorium

As far as pop culture is concerned, a vomitorium is a room where ancient Romans went to throw up lavish meals so they could return to the table and feast some more. It's a striking illustration of gluttony and waste, and one that makes its way into modern texts. Suzanne Collins' "The Hunger Games" series, for example, alludes to vomitoriums when the lavish inhabitants of the Capitol—all with Latin names like Flavia and Octavia—imbibe a drink to make them vomit at parties so they can gorge themselves on more calories than citizens in the surrounding districts would see in months

But the real story behind vomitoriums is much less disgusting. Actual ancient Romans did love food and drink. But even the wealthiest did not have special rooms for purging. To Romans, vomitoriums were the entrances/exits in stadiums or theaters, so dubbed by a fifth-century writer because of the way they'd spew crowds out into the streets.

"It's just kind of a trope," that ancient Romans were luxurious and vapid enough to engage in rituals of binging and purging, said Sarah Bond, an assistant professor of classics at the University of Iowa.

ABOUT THE AUTHOR

David Bobker is a prolific author who has published over 30 books under several pen names. His purpose as an author is to enlighten and help people through his books.

Previously David has been an Advisory Director at Argyle, Senior Vice President of AST Phoenix Advisors, Managing Director with Georgeson and was one of the founders of Laurel Hill Advisors.

A 1993 graduate of the City University of New York's Brooklyn College with a Bachelor's degree in Computer Science, David earned his MBA in Marketing and Finance from the City University of New York's Baruch College in 2000. David lives with his wife Shoshana, a certified nutritionist, and their seven children in Passaic, New Jersey.

www.ingramcontent.com/pod-product-compliance
Lightning Source LLC
Chambersburg PA
CBHW030410160726
47992CB00007B/3056